What Is That?

WRITTEN & ILLUSTRATED BY
SANDRA HARMON

Text and illustrations ©2024 Sandra Harmon. All Rights Reserved. No part of this publication may be reproduced, stored in a retrieval system, or transmitted in any form or by any means—electronic, mechanical, photocopy, recording, or any other—except for brief quotations in printed reviews, without the prior permission from the publisher.

Published by Sandy's Shelf Books
www.SandysShelf.com
SandysShelf@conciergemarketing.com

Hardcover: 978-1-961153-04-2
Paperback: 978-1-961153-05-9

Library of Congress Cataloging Number and
Cataloging in Publication Data on file with publisher.

Production and design by Concierge Marketing Publishing Services.
Printed in the United States of America.

10 9 8 7 6 5 4 3 2 1

This book is dedicated to the 4-H, FFA, Scouts
and all the clubs and organizations
that help young people to become the best they can be.

"Elly, Grandma Sarah would like you to come for another visit," said Elly's mom, Shelley.

"Does she need help with her dogs , cats, pigs, horses, and bird? Or maybe she has more animals to show me," Elly said excitedly.

Elly's dad, Brian, laughed, shook, his head and said. "Not this time, Pumpkin."

"PUMPKIN?" Why did you call me that? Do I look round and orange to you?" asked Elly.

"No, Grandma Sarah liked to call some of her children that when they were little. I said it just for fun," chuckled Brian.

"Pack a suitcase," Shelley told her little girl." We will probably stay for a week."

As they drove to Grandma's house, Elly had many ideas about why Grandma Sarah wanted her to come.

Freckles, the dog, and Gracie the cat, greeted the family as they got out of the car. Elly gave each of them a big hug. "I'll hug the others later." smiled Elly.

"Come in and have some cookies. I want to tell you all about the county Fair," said Grandma Sarah.

"A county Fair? What is that?" questioned Elly as she ate her yummy cookie.

Grandma started to explain,"Each summer some of my family, friends and neighbors get together to enter contests at the county Fair. We enter animals we've raised on the farm, vegetables or fruit we've grown. We can enter things we've baked like bread, pies, or…"

"Or COOKIES!" shouted Elly.

"Yes, cookies," laughed Grandma Sarah.

Some people like to enter crafts or artwork, like things they have sewn, clever gadgets and other things they've made, photograghs, drawings and paintings," Shelley added.

"There will also be lots of things to do, food to eat, games to play and they even crown a County Fair Queen."

Elly asks, "How do you know about a county Fair?"

"We would go to the Fair when we were kids," Shelley answered.

"Now it's time for you to go to one, too," Grandma said.

Uncle Denny came in and asked, "Want to help me shampoo the pigs?"

"Why do they need a bath? Pigs are usually muddy. Do they like a bath? I thought pigs liked to be muddy." Elly wondered.

"Enough questions Elly" said Uncle Denny, "I am taking them to the county Fair. I need to wash off the dirt and the purple stain they got from being under the mulberry tree,"

"These pigs love their bath." laughed Elly.

Uncle Denny replied, "Pigs really don't try to be dirty. The cool mud helps to keep them from getting too hot on these warm summer days. Thanks for your help, Elly"

As she headed back to the house, Elly saw Roger and Barb with their horses. "Are you taking them to the Fair? Will the horses get ribbons for how pretty they look?"

Barb smiled and said, "They are pretty, but we are riding them in a parade before the Fair starts."

So much to see at a county Fair," Elly mused as she heads back to the house.

Riley was putting her guinea pigs Mars and Venus in a cage so they could go to the Fair.

Elly could smell the wonderful aroma of the cookies Grandma Sarah was baking.

Shelley looked up from her sewing and said, "Don't bother Grandma right now; she's making those cookies for the County Fair."

"What a cute little dress you're making. Is it for me?" Elly asks. "Maybe later you can wear it, but first it will be entered at the Fair." Shelley replied.

"Is Daddy entering anything?" Elly asks.

"Not this year, Elly" Brian says with a smile. "The Fair is not just for earning awards. I am going to help with a display about scouting. When I was your age, I was a Boy Scout. We are making a display to show how scouts help people, learn things, and just have fun."

"Elly, I have fun news for you. Your teacher told me students from her class may enter artwork they have made at school. Would you like to do that?" said Shelley. "Your cousin Madge is entering some artwork."

"Oh, what fun. Yes, I want to show my artwork. I'll let my teacher know which ones to take to the Fair."

Early on the first day of the Fair everyone helped to pack things they made, and loaded the animals they were taking.

At the Fairgrounds, a parade kicked off start of the County Fair.

There were all kinds of tractors, trucks, and cars with signs on them, and firetrucks.

Then came the horses. Barb was riding Trixie, and Roger was riding Sugar Babe.

I can't wait till I'm big enough to ride a horse, too, Elly thought.

As Elly looked around, she saw carnival rides and fun games in the midway, and she saw big tents and big buildings with big doors.

In one of the big buildings, there were rows and rows of tables and lots of art hanging on the walls. Elly found her artwork and the pictures Madge had made. It was exciting to see her art hanging where many people could see it.

At the other end of the building was a display of sewing entries and other crafts. Elly smiled as she saw the pretty little dress her mother Shelley had made.

Other buildings had all kinds of farm animals. Little feathered ones like chickens and ducks. Little furry ones like rabbits and guinea pigs. There Elly found Riley with her guinea pigs, Mars and Venus.

A really large building had cattle. Jeremy, Grandma Sarah's neighbor, was working with the calf I saw on my last visit to Grandma's. The calf was a lot smaller then!

In another building were goats and sheep. Jeremy joined me and introduced me to his friend McCoy. McCoy had brought lambs to the Fair. I wished them good luck.

Elly saw some pretty girls dressed in gowns. Why would they wear such fancy dresses here?

Then she heard someone announce "It's time to crown the queen."

"Silly Elly," she thought to herself "I forgot Dad told me there would be a County Fair Queen." Elly arrived just as last year's queen placed the crown on the new queen. Smiling to herself, Elly thought, *maybe someday I can be the queen.*

What else is at a Fair?

Brian waved to Elly. He was sitting in a little tent, pretending he was camping with the scouts.

Uncle Howard had joined them. Howard had been a scout, too. He was delighting the scouts with funny stories.

Later he will be part of the Fair's entertainment playing his guitar and singing songs.

Everyone was getting hungry. There are so many things one could choose. Tacos, hot dogs, hamburgers, BBQ sandwiches, chips, popcorn, cookies, ice cream, and many different things to drink.

The Fair lasted several days.

Finally, the day came when the judges awarded the ribbons for all the entries.

1st – Blue
2nd – Red
3rd – White
4th – Yellow
5th – Green
6th – Pink
Champion – Purple

Elly first found Riley. One guinea pig got a red ribbon, the other blue. (I will let you guess which one got the blue ribbon. Was it Mars or Venus?)

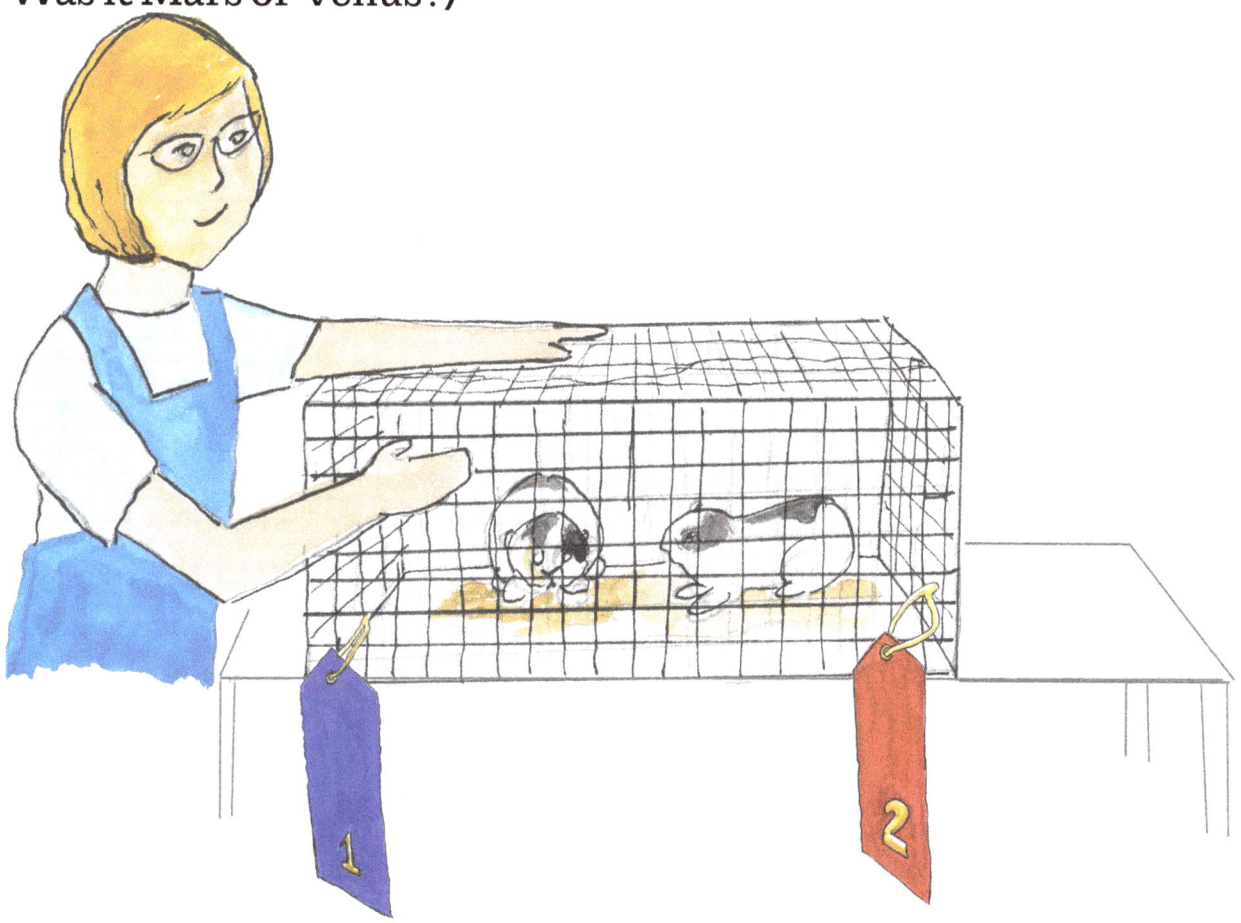

A blue ribbon was on the pretty little Elly dress that her mom had made. Elly gave her mom a big hug.

Madge was waiting for her by the artwork. She had a red ribbon and a pink ribbon. She was incredibly happy because they were her favorite colors.

Ribbons were on Elly's art, too. One was red and one was blue. She was very happy about the 1st place blue, but red was her favorite color, too.

A blue ribbon was on Grandma Sarah's chocolate chip cookies, of course.

McCoy and Jeremy received ribbons, too. What color do you think their animals got?

Almost time to go home, but what about Uncle Denny's pigs?

The pigs were purple again, not from mulberries. They had won GRAND CHAMPION purple ribbons!!!!

At the Fair, Elly saw signs that said 4-H and FFA.

Elly said, "I know what a county Fair is but what are 4-H and FFA?"

"Let's see if I can explain." replied Shelley. 4-H helps young people to learn to be leaders through camps, clubs, and afterschool programs. The 4 H's stand for Head, Heart, Hands, and Health.

FFA stands for Future Farmer of America.

They prepare kids to be leaders and have jobs in agriculture (the running of a farm.)

Many of the entries at the Fair are from these two groups.

This book is dedicated to the 4-H, FFA, Scouts

and all the clubs and organizations

that help young people to become the best they can be.

What would you enter at the County Fair?

THE END

www.ingramcontent.com/pod-product-compliance
Lightning Source LLC
Chambersburg PA
CBHW062023050526
44107CB00106B/978